The Cola Cookbook

Get Cooking with Cola! From Casseroles to Cupcakes, and More

BY

Christina Tosch

Copyright Notes

Table of Contents

Introduction

Flavor your food with one of the world's favorite soft drinks. All you need is a creative cookbook and a can of cola!

You can use any brand of cola you like; no one make is preferable to any other. All you have to remember is the cola should be room temperature and, unless specified, always use regular cola with sugar rather than diet. Diet cola can sometimes taste bitter when cooked.

What's more, it's a great way to use up flat cola, too.

You will be pleasantly surprised just how much of a difference a simple cup of cola can make to everyday family recipes.

The recipes in the Cola Cookbook will show you how to use flavored, regular and diet cola to infuse and add flavor to grilled meats, fish, pasta, veggies, fruit, and more.

Go beyond the can and check out the best 40 sweet and savory recipes in the Cola Cookbook today!

Appetizers Lite Bites

Arroz Con Cola

Rice is South American staple and often enjoyed alone as simple, tasty meal or side. This flavorsome rice cooked in cola makes a yummy lunch or can even be served as a side with your favourite cola main dishes.

Servings: 4

Total Time: 30min

Ingredients:

- 1 cup long-grain white rice (rinsed)
- 1½ cups cola
- 1 cup water
- 3 tbsp scallions (chopped)
- 2 tbsp butter
- 1 chick bouillon cube

Directions:

1. Add the rice, cola, water, scallions, butter, and bouillon cube to a saucepan over moderately high heat and bring to a boil. Stir once then cover and turn the heat down low. Cook for 20 minutes.

2. Take the pan off the heat and set to one side for 5 minutes.

3. Take off the lid and fluff the rice before serving.

Bacon-Wrapped Scallops

Soaking juicy scallops in cola will add flavor and pair perfectly with salty bacon, tangy ketchup, and smoked paprika seasoning while water chestnuts will add a crisp texture.

Servings: 4

Total Time: 2hours 35min

Ingredients:

- 8 rashers medium-cut bacon (cut in half)
- Cola (room temperature, as needed)
- 16 sea scallops (rinsed, patted dry)
- Sea salt (to season)
- 1 (8 ounces) can water chestnuts (drained)
- 1 tbsp smoked paprika
- ¼ cup ketchup

Directions:

1. Arrange the bacon in a container and pour in enough cola to cover. Cover and place in the fridge for 2 hours.

2. Season the scallops lightly with sea salt and set aside for 10 minutes.

3. Preheat the main oven to 425 degrees F.

4. Remove the bacon from the cola, shaking off any excess.

5. Place one seasoned scallop in the middle of one slice of bacon and top with a water chestnut.

6. Roll the bacon over to cover and secure with a cocktail stick.

7. Season with paprika and baste with ketchup.

8. Bake in the preheated oven for 25-30 minutes, depending on the thickness of the bacon.

9. Serve and enjoy.

Jalapeño and Bacon Shrimp with Homemade Cherry Cola Barbue Sauce

If you are a seafood fan, you will love these tasty bacon-wrapped jumbo shrimp served with a sweet and tart cherry cola BBQ sauce.

Servings: 16

Total Time: 40min

Ingredients:

- 1½ tbsp. bacon drippings
- 1 cup red onion (peeled, chopped)
- 2 cloves garlic (peeled, chopped)
- ½ tsp sea salt
- ¼ tsp dry mustard
- ½ tsp garlic powder
- 2 cups cherry cola (room temperature)
- ½ cup red wine vinegar
- 1 cup ketchup

Shrimp

- 16 jumbo shrimp (peeled, deveined, tails removed)
- 1 jalapeno (stemmed, seeded, thinly sliced into 16 strips)
- 8 slices bacon (halved crosswise)
- 1 tsp sea salt
- 1 tsp black pepper

Directions:

1. For the BBQ sauce: Over moderate-high heat, in a pan heat the bacon drippings.

2. Add the onion to the pan. Cook while stirring occasionally for 5 minutes, or until softened. Next, add the garlic and cook while frequently stirring for 60 seconds.

3. Stir in the sea salt followed by the mustard and garlic powder and cook, while frequently stirring for 2 minutes, or until the spices are fragrant, toasted, and the onion is a rich maroon color.

4. Whisk in the cola and red wine vinegar, and while stirring often, cook for approximately 2 minutes.

5. Finally, stir in the ketchup and bring to boil. Cook until the mixture easily coats the back of a spoon and is reduced. This step will take 12-15 minutes.

6. In the meantime, prepare the shrimp. Over moderate heat, heat a skillet.

7. Make a ¼" deep, long slit in the inner curve of each jumbo shrimp. Place 1 strip of jalapeno into the slit.

8. Wrap each shrimp tightly with 1 slice of bacon. Arrange on a platter, seam side facing downwards. Season lightly.

9. Put the wrapped shrimp, seam sides facing downwards in the hot pan, and while occasionally turning, cook for 5-6 minutes, or until the shrimp are cooked through, and the bacon is crisp.

10. Serve the shrimp alongside the sauce and enjoy.

Black Bean Soup

Enjoy this easy-to-make satisfying black bean soup made with cola makes a mouth-watering meal.

Servings: 8

Total Time: 1hour 40min

Ingredients:

- 1 pound dried black beans (rinsed, drained)
- 8-10 cups ham stock
- 1 (12 ounces) can cola (room temperature)
- Freshly squeezed juice of ½ lime
- 1 tsp ground cumin
- 1 tsp ground coriander
- Sour cream (to serve)
- Fresh cilantro (chopped)
- 1 avocado (peeled, pitted, and diced)
- Wedges of lime

Directions:

1. Add the beans to a large pan. Pour in 8 cups of the ham stock and cola and bring to boil. Partially cover the pan and reduce the heat to low. Stir in the lime juice, cumin, and coriander. Cook until the black beans are bite-tender, for 1½ hours. Add additional stock as necessary.

2. Using an immersion blender, blend the soup until you achieve a thick puree-like consistency while leaving some of the beans partly intact. Taste and season.

3. Serve your soup in bowls, with a swirl of sour cream, a sprinkling of cilantro, and a spoonful of diced avocado. Serve with fresh wedges of lime for squeezing.

Chicken Cola Hot Wings

Dip these cola and hot sauce chicken wings in a creamy blue cheese dressing and enjoy.

Servings: 30

Total Time: 45min

Ingredients:

- 3 pounds chicken wings
- 1 cup hot sauce
- 1 tbsp soy sauce
- 1 (12 ounces) can cola (room temperature)
- ¼ tsp black pepper
- ¼ tsp cayenne pepper
- Blue cheese dressing (store-bought, as needed)

Directions:

1. Cut the wings into 3 sections. Discard the wingtips.

2. In a bowl, combine the hot sauce with the soy sauce, cola, black pepper, and cayenne. Stir to combine.

3. Prepare your grill using a drip pan for indirect heat. Covered, grill the wings over indirect moderate heat on an oiled grill rack for 10 minutes. Grill for an additional 30-40 minutes while occasionally turning, and frequently basting until the wings are glazed.

4. Serve with the blue cheese dressing.

Cola French Onion Soup

French onion soup is the ideal lite-bite to serve with crusty bread. What's more, it's ready in less than one hour.

Servings: 4

Total Time: 55min

Ingredients:

- ¼ cup butter
- 4 cups onions (peeled, thinly sliced)
- 4 cups beef broth
- 14 ounces water
- ¾ cup cola (room temperature)
- 1 tsp salt
- ⅛ tsp black pepper
- Croutons (to serve)
- 4 slices Swiss cheese
- Parmesan cheese (freshly grated)
- Crusty bread (to serve)

Directions:

1. In a pan, melt the butter. Add the onions to the pan. Cook until golden. Do not brown.

2. Add the beef broth (undiluted) along with water, the cola, salt, and black pepper. Cover and simmer for 20-25 minutes.

3. Ladle into soup bowls and add the croutons.

4. Top with Swiss cheese and scatter freshly grated Parmesan over the top.

5. Microwave for 20-25 seconds until the cheese is melted.

6. Serve with crusty bread.

Hawaiian Cola Turkey Sandwiches

The star of the show in the delicious artisanal sandwiches is the creamy sweet and spicy cola sauce.

Servings: 6

Total Time: 35min

Ingredients:

Turkey:

- 1 cup cola (room temperature)
- ¼ cup low-sodium soy sauce
- ¼ cup olive oil
- 4 cloves garlic (peeled, minced)
- ¼ tsp freshly ground black pepper
- Nonstick cooking spray
- 2 pounds turkey breast, boneless, skinless (cut into long strips)

Sauce:

- ¾ cup mayonnaise
- 2 tbsp honey
- 2 tbsp sweet chili sauce
- ¼ tsp freshly ground black pepper
- 1 tsp hot sauce

Sandwiches:

- 6 hot dog buns
- Head of romaine lettuce
- 1 cup fresh pineapple (coarsely chopped)
- ¼ cup cilantro (chopped)
- Black pepper (to season)

Directions:

1. In a bowl, whisk the cola with the soy sauce, olive oil, garlic, and black pepper. Pour the mixture over the turkey. Cover with kitchen wrap and transfer to the fridge to marinate for a minimum of 2 hours.

2. In the meantime, prepare the sauce.

3. In a bowl, combine the sauce ingredients (mayonnaise, honey, chili sauce, black pepper, and hot sauce) and whisk until incorporated. Transfer to the fridge until you are ready to serve.

4. Spritz a grill pan with nonstick cooking spray and heat over moderate heat.

5. In batches to avoid overcrowding the pan, cook the turkey for approximately 5 minutes on each side, or until the meat registers an internal temperature of 170 degrees F.

6. To assemble: Thinly slice the turkey. Cut the buns crosswise in half. Arrange a lettuce leaf inside each bun, top with turkey followed by pineapple. Drizzle with mayonnaise sauce, garnish with chopped cilantro, and season with pepper.

Shredded Beef Sandwiches

Cola is the secret ingredient in these delicious, slow-cooked beef sandwiches.

Servings: 8

Total Time: 8hours 20min

Ingredients:

- ¾ cup cola (room temperature)
- ¼ cup Worcestershire sauce
- 2 cloves garlic (peeled, minced)
- 1 tbsp white vinegar
- 1 tsp reduced-sodium beef bouillon granules
- ½ tsp chili powder
- ½ tsp ground mustard
- ¼ tsp cayenne pepper
- 1 (2 pounds) rump roast
- 2 tsp canola oil
- 2 medium-size onions (peeled, chopped)
- ½ cup ketchup
- 8 hoagie buns (split)

Directions:

1. In a measuring cup, combine the cola with the Worcestershire sauce, garlic, white vinegar, beef bouillon granules, chili powder, ground mustard, and cayenne pepper. Put aside.

2. Cut the rump roast in half.

3. In a pan, heat the oil, add the beef to the pan and brown all over.

4. Add the onions to a slow cooker or 3-quart capacity.

5. Pour approximately half of the cola mixture over the beef. Cover, and on low, cook for 8-10 hours until the meat is fork-tender.

6. Cover and place the remaining cola mixture in the fridge.

7. Remove the beef from the cooking liquid and allow to cool. Strain the cooking liquid. Reserve the onions and discard the cooking liquid.

8. When the beef is cooled enough to handle, using metal forks, shred. Return the shredded meat to the slow cooker.

9. In a bowl, combine the ketchup with the reserved cola mixture and pour it over the meat. Heat through and serve on hoagie buns.

Slow Cooker Cola Chicken Nachos

Loaded chicken nachos are a movie night in, hassle-free lite bite to share.

Servings: 6-8

Total Time: 4hour 10min

Ingredients:

- 2 pounds chicken breast (diced or sliced)
- 1 cup tomato ketchup
- ½ onion (peeled, diced)
- 1 cup cola (room temperature)
- Nachos (to serve)
- Tomatoes (chopped, to serve)
- Guacamole (to serve)
- Cheese (shredded, to serve)

Directions:

1. Add the chicken to a slow cooker. Top with the ketchup, onion, and cola. Gently stir to combine.

2. Cook for 4 hours on high or until cooked through.

3. Shred the chicken and spoon it over the nachos.

4. Top with chopped tomatoes, guacamole, and shredded cheese.

Mains

BBQ Cola Ribs

Finger-lickin' good, these sticky sweet ribs with BBQ cola glaze are the perfect game day or movie night snack.

Servings: 4

Total Time: 9hours 15min

Ingredients:

- Butter (to grease)
- ¼ cup brown sugar
- 1 tsp salt
- ½ tsp black pepper
- 2 cloves garlic (peeled, minced)
- 3 tbsp liquid smoke
- 4 pounds pork spareribs (cut into smaller pieces)
- 1 onion (peeled, thinly sliced)
- ½ cup cola(room temperature)
- 1½ cups BBQ sauce (of choice)

Directions:

1. Grease a slow cooker insert with butter.

2. Combine the brown sugar, salt, black pepper, garlic, and liquid smoke in a bowl.

3. Rub the mixture evenly into the ribs. Arrange the onion and ribs in the slow cooker. Pour over the cola and cook for 8-10 hours on low heat until the ribs are tender. Drain away any liquid from the slow cooker.

4. Pour the cola and BBQ sauce over the ribs and cook for one more hour. Allow to rest for 10 minutes before serving.

Big Beefy Chili

Packed fully with beef and Ranch-style beans, this tasty chili will fill even the hungriest of tummies.

Servings: 8

Total Time: 2hours

Ingredients:

- 2 pounds ground beef
- 3 cloves garlic (peeled, minced)
- 1 onion (peeled, diced)
- 2 tsp cumin
- 2 tbsp chili powder
- 1 tbsp salt
- 2 bay leaves
- 1 tsp black pepper
- ½ cup beef stock
- 12 ounces diet cola (room temperature)
- 1 (28 ounces) can diced tomatoes
- 1 (14 ounces) can Ranch-style beans (drained, rinsed)
- White rice (cooked, to serve)

Directions:

1. In a stockpot over moderately high heat, sauté the beef, garlic, and onion until browned.

2. Stir in the cumin, chili powder, salt, bay leaves, black pepper, beef stock, diet cola, canned tomatoes, and beans.

3. Bring the chili to a boil then turn down to a simmer. Cook for 1–1½ hours until thick and flavorful.

4. Serve with white rice.

Braised Cola Onions and Sausage

Re-create this childhood favorite with cola and serve on a bed of creamy mash.

Servings: 4

Total Time: 35min

Ingredients:

- 1 tbsp extra-virgin olive oil
- 2 sweet onions (peeled, thinly sliced)
- Salt and black pepper
- 1 cup cola (room temperature)
- 2 tbsp honey
- 4 fresh thyme sprigs
- 8 cooked, store-bought chicken and apple sausages
- Mashed potatoes (to serve, optional)

Directions:

1. Preheat your main oven to 375 degrees F.

2. In a Dutch oven over moderate heat, heat the oil.

3. Add the onions and season with salt and black pepper. Cook until tender, for 3-5 minutes.

4. Pour in the cola and add the honey and sprigs of thyme stirring to coat the onions evenly. Cook for an additional 5 minutes.

5. Nestle the cooked sausage over the top and in-between the onions and transfer to the oven to cook for 20-25 minutes.

6. Remove from the oven and serve the sausage with the onions and a helping of creamy mash.

Brown Sugar Cola Glazed Ham

This spiral ham is coated in a brown sugar and sweet cola glaze. It is baked to mouth-watering perfection and makes an ideal special occasion main.

Servings: 16-18

Total Time: 2hours 20min

Ingredients:

- Nonstick cooking spray
- 1 (10 pounds) spiral ham
- ½ cup brown sugar
- 1 (12 ounces) cola (room temperature)
- 1 tbsp cornstarch (optional)
- 2 tbsp cold water (optional)

Directions:

1. Preheat the main oven to 350 degrees F.

2. Spritz a roasting pan with nonstick cooking spray.

3. Place the ham in the roasting pan. Rub the brown sugar evenly all over the ham, making sure it reaches in between the slices.

4. Pour the cola over the ham, cover and bake in the oven for 1½ hours. You will need to baste every half hour.

5. Uncover and bake for an additional 30 minutes or more until the ham is caramelized and browned.

6. Remove the ham from the roasting pan and transfer to a platter.

7. Spoon the glaze from the bottom of the roasting pan over the ham.

8. If you need to thicken the glaze, pour the glaze from the pan into a small pot and bring to simmer.

9. In a small bowl, whisk the cornstarch with the water. Pour the slurry into the pot, while continually whisking. Bring to boil and cook for 60 seconds, until thickened.

Cola-Battered Fried Fish with Lemon Dill Dipping Sauce

Banish the beer and batter fresh fish with fizzy cola. It really helps to bring out the sweet flavor of the tilapia.

Servings: 2

Total Time: 1hour

Ingredients:

Fish:

- 1½ cups all-purpose flour (divided)
- 1½ cups cornmeal (divided)
- 1 tsp baking powder
- 1 tbsp seasoned salt
- 1 tbsp freshly ground black pepper
- 1½ cups cola (room temperature)
- 3 cups canola oil (to fry)
- 1 pound tilapia fillets
- 2 jalapenos (thinly sliced)

Lemon Dill Dipping Sauce:

- ½ cup sour cream
- ½ cup mayonnaise
- Juice of ½ a lemon
- 1 tsp dill
- 1 tsp salt

Directions:

1. In a bowl, combine a cup of flour with a cup of cornmeal, baking powder, salt, black pepper, and cola. Transfer to the fridge for 10 minutes.

2. In a second bowl, mix the remaining flour with the cornmeal.

3. In a frying pan over moderate-high heat, heat the oil to a minimum of 350 degrees F.

4. In the meantime, remove the batter from Step 1 from the fridge.

5. In batches of 2 or 3, dredge the fish and jalapeño in the dry mixture, and then in the batter.

6. Once the oil is sufficiently hot, fry the fish and jalapenos for approximately 30-60 seconds on each side, until golden.

7. For the dipping sauce: In a bowl, whisk the sour cream with the mayonnaise, fresh lemon juice, dill, and salt. Taste and adjust the seasoning.

8. Serve the battered fish with the dipping sauce.

Crock Pot Cola Venison Roast

This crock pot cola vension roast is a mouth-watering meal to come home to. The sugar in the cola does a great job of tenderizing the meat.

Servings: 4

Total Time: 6hours 10min

Ingredients:

- 1 large onion (peeled, sliced)
- 1 pounds venison roast
- 1 (12 ounces) can cola (room temperature)
- 14 ounces tomato ketchup

Directions:

1. Add the onions to a crockpot.

2. Place the venison roast on top of the onions.

3. In a mixing bowl, combine the cola with the ketchup until well blended. Pour the mixture over the roast.

4. Cover, and on low, cook for 6-8 hours until medium-rare. Overcooking venison can lead to the meat becoming dry and tough.

Meat 'n Potato Cola Kabobs with Pineapple

Fizzy cola is a great and inexpensive marinade for all sorts of meat, including beef and chicken.

Servings: 4

Total Time: 25min

Ingredients:

- 1½ tsp steak seasoning (divided)
- 1 clove garlic (peeled, minced)
- 1 cup cola (room temperature)
- 1 pound beef top sirloin steak (cut into 1" cubes)
- 3 small-size red potatoes (cubed)
- 1 tbsp water
- 1 sweet orange pepper (cut into 1" pieces)
- 1 tsp canola oil
- 1 cup pineapple chunks
- 1 cup cherry tomatoes

Directions:

1. Season the beef with 1 teaspoon of steak seasoning and sprinkle over the minced garlic.

2. Pour the cola into a large Ziploc bag.

3. Add the seasoned beef and garlic to the bag and toss gently to coat. Put to one side.

4. In a microwave-safe bowl, combine the potatoes with the water and covered, microwave on high for 4-5 minutes, until just tender. Return to the bowl and add the tomatoes along with the sweet orange pepper, oil, and the remaining steak seasoning. Toss to coat.

5. Drain the meat and discard the marinade.

6. Using 8 skewers, thread the beef, veggies, and pineapple. Grill, while covered over moderate heat for 6-8 minutes until the meat reaches your preferred level of doneness, and the pepper is tender-crisp. You will need to occasionally turn the skewers during cooking.

7. Serve and enjoy.

Next Recipe

Mini Meatballs in a Sweet and Spicy Sauce

Succulent beef meatballs sit in a rich and flavorsome sauce infused with cinnamon sugar, cherry cola, and garlic. You'll never crave ordinary meatballs again!

Servings: 3-4

Total Time: 55min

Ingredients:

Sauce:

- 12 ounces cherry cola (room temperature)
- 1 cup tomato ketchup
- 3 tbsp tomato paste
- 1 tbsp soy sauce
- 2 tbsp cinnamon cane sugar
- 1 tsp powdered garlic

Meatballs:

- 1 pound ground chuck beef
- ½ cup Italian breadcrumbs
- 1 egg (beaten)
- ½ cup Parmesan cheese (grated)
- 1 tsp onion powder
- 1 tsp powdered garlic
- ½ tsp salt
- ½ tsp black pepper
- Pasta of choice (cooked, to serve)

Directions:

1. Preheat a main oven to 350 degrees F. Cover a baking sheet with parchment paper.

2. Add the cola, tomato ketchup, tomato paste, soy sauce, sugar, and garlic to a saucepan and whisk to combine. Set to one side to use later.

3. Combine the ground beef, breadcrumbs, beaten egg, grated cheese, onion powder, powdered garlic, salt, and black pepper in a bowl using clean hands.

4. Roll the mixture into 24 equally-sized balls and arrange on the baking sheet. Place in the oven and bake for just over 20 minutes until cooked through.

5. Place the set aside saucepan over moderate heat. Transfer the cooked meatballs to the saucepan and cook for 10 minutes while basting the meatballs with the sauce. When hot through, serve with your pasta of choice.

One-Skillet Mushroom Chicken

This versatile chicken dish can be served with rice, noodles, pasta, or even potatoes. What's more, made using only one skillet, you don't have to worry about time-consuming washing up afterward!

Servings: 4

Total Time: 40min

Ingredients:

- 4 chicken thighs
- Salt and black pepper
- 3 tbsp olive oil
- 8 ounces mushrooms (chopped)
- 2 shallots (diced)
- 4 cloves garlic (peeled, minced)
- 5 tbsp flour
- 1 cup chicken broth
- 2 (12 ounces) cans cola (room temperature)
- 1 bay leaf
- Fresh parsley (chopped, to garnish)

Directions:

1. Season the chicken thighs with salt and black pepper.

2. Warm the oil in a skillet over moderately high heat, add the chicken and sauté on all sides until evenly golden. Take the chicken out of the skillet and set to one side.

3. To the same skillet, add the mushrooms and shallots, sauté until softened. Add the garlic and sauté for 60 more seconds.

4. Whisk in the flour followed by the chicken broth and cola. When no lumps remain, add the bay leaf.

5. Return the chicken to the skillet and turn the heat down to moderately low. Bring to a simmer and cook for approximately half an hour or until the chicken is cooked through.

6. Garnish with fresh parsley before serving.

Pulled Pork with Cherry Cola BBQ Sauce

Who doesn't love classic pulled pork served in a brioche bun?! This crockpot recipe can be thrown together in the morning with a minimum of fuss and be enjoyed in the evening.

Servings: 6

Total Time: 8hours 10min

Ingredients:

- 2 tsp red pepper flakes
- 1 tbsp salt
- 1 tbsp black pepper
- 4 pounds pork tenderloin
- BBQ sauce (of choice)
- 1 (12 ounces) can cherry cola (room temperature)
- 6 brioche buns (toasted)

Directions:

1. In a small bowl, combine the crushed red pepper flakes, salt, and black pepper. Rub the mixture evenly onto the outside of the pork.

2. Place the pork in your crockpot. Brush the pork all over with BBQ sauce. Pour over the can of cherry cola. Cook for 8 hours on low heat.

3. Toast the brioche buns.

4. Allow to rest for 10 minutes before dividing between the brioche buns and serving.

Slow-Cooked Steak Stroganoff

Adding cola to this recipe brings a subtle sweetness to a classic meaty stew. With a creamy sauce and chunks of tender sirloin steak, stroganoff is a hearty dinner the whole family will enjoy.

Servings: 16

Total Time: 8hours 15min

Ingredients:

- 4 pounds beef top sirloin steak (cubed)
- 1 pound fresh mushrooms (sliced)
- 2 (14½ ounces) cans chicken broth
- ½ cup yellow onion (diced)
- 1 (12 ounces) can cola (room temperature)
- 1½ tsp garlic powder
- 1 (1.8 ounces) sachet instant onion soup mix
- 2 tsp dried parsley
- ½ tsp black pepper
- 1 (2.6 ounces) sachet country gravy mix
- 2 cups sour cream
- Egg noodles (cooked, to serve)

Directions:

1. Combine the steak, mushrooms, chicken broth, onion, cola, garlic, onion soup mix, parsley, and black pepper in a slow cooker.

2. Cook on low heat for 7-8 hours.

3. Use a slotted spoon, remove the mushrooms and beef from the slow cooker and set to one side.

4. Pour the remaining sauce into a saucepan along with the country gravy mix, whisk to combine, and bring to a boil while stirring for 2 minutes. When the sauce is thick, take off the heat. Fold in the sour cream.

5. Return the mushrooms and steak to the sauce and serve with cooked egg noodles.

Spicy Pecan Salmon

Chopped pecans are toasted and combined with sweet cola, and spicy Tabasco for a unique and yummy sauce, your friends will definitely beg you for this recipe!

Servings: 4

Total Time: 30min

Ingredients:

- 4 salmon fillets, skinless
- 1 tbsp canola oil
- ½ cup pecans (chopped)
- 12 ounces cola (room temperature)
- 1 tbsp butter
- 1 tbsp Tabasco sauce

Directions:

1. Brush the salmon fillets with oil then set to one side.

2. In a skillet over moderate heat, toast the pecans until browned. Take the pecans out of the skillet and set aside.

3. Pour the cola into the skillet and bring to a boil, turn down to a simmer. Heat until the cola has reduced by half and is thick and syrupy.

4. Stir in the butter and Tabasco. Return the pecans to the skillet. Stir to combine and keep warm.

5. Grill the salmon fillets for 3-4 minutes on each side until cooked through.

6. Serve the salmon with the sauce over the top and enjoy.

Sticky Asian Sesame Chicken

An Asian-inspired main made at home with fresh ingredients will always beat a greasy take-out. And ready in less than 30 minutes, you can be enjoying this tasty meal before the delivery guy even makes it to your door!

Servings: 2

Total Time: 55min

Ingredients:

- ½ tbsp sesame oil
- 4 cloves garlic (peeled, grated)
- 1 inch chunk fresh ginger (peeled, grated)
- 4 chicken thigh fillets (diced)
- White pepper
- 1 cup cola (room temperature)
- Soy sauce
- 1 tbsp toasted sesame seeds
- White rice (steamed, to serve)

Directions:

1. In a skillet over moderate heat, warm the sesame oil. Add the garlic and ginger and sauté until the ingredients sizzle.

2. Add the chicken to the skillet along with a pinch of white pepper, stir to combine until browned. Remove the chicken and set to one side.

3. Pour the cola into the skillet. Turn the heat up to high, then cook until the cola reduces by half and becomes syrupy.

4. Turn the heat down low and return the chicken to the skillet and season with soy sauce to taste. Cook until the sauce thickens up a little more.

5. Scatter over the sesame seeds just before serving with white rice.

Tangy Baked Pork Chops

With just 4 ingredients, these tender, baked pork chops could not be easier to throw together. Zero stress and maximum flavor, what's not to love?!

Servings: 2

Total Time: 45min

Ingredients:

- Nonstick cooking spray
- 2 (5 ounces) boneless pork loin chops
- 8 red onion rings
- ¼ cup tomato ketchup
- ¼ cup cola (room temperature)
- Mashed potatoes (hot, to serve)

Directions:

1. Preheat a main oven to 350 degrees F. Spritz a baking dish with nonstick cooking spray.

2. Arrange the pork chops in the baking dish and arrange the onion rings on top.

3. In a small bowl, stir together the tomato ketchup and cola. Pour the mixture over the chops.

4. Place in the oven, then bake for 35-40 minutes or until cooked through.

5. Serve hot with mashed potatoes.

Weekend Casserole

What could be easier than this beefy casserole? Prep the veggies, pop them in a pot, and hey presto you have a satisfying weekend family-friendly meal.

Servings: 6

Total Time: 1hour 15min

Ingredients:

- 1½ tbsp oil
- 1 large-size onion (peeled, sliced)
- 1 pound ground beef
- ¼ cup rice (uncooked)
- 2-3 celery stalks (chopped)
- 1 green bell pepper (chopped)
- 1 (15 ounces) can kidney beans (drained)
- 1 (14 ounces) can tomato soup
- 1 (12 ounces) can cola (room temperature)

Directions:

1. Swirl the oil around the bottom of a 9x13" casserole dish.

2. Layer the ingredients into the dish in recipe order; onion, beef, rice, celery, bell pepper, kidney beans, and tomato soup. Pour the cola evenly over the top.

3. Cover with aluminum foil and bake in the oven at 350 degrees F for 60 minutes.

4. Enjoy.

Desserts Sweet Treats

Candy Cola Bark

Made with low-calorie ingredients, this cherry cola candy bark is the perfect one-serving treat to help beat those sugary cravings.

Servings: 1

Total Time: 2hours 10min

Ingredients:

- 2 tbsp frozen cherries (chopped)
- 1 tbsp coconut oil
- ½ tbsp cocoa powder, unsweetened
- 1-2 drops cola-flavor liquid sweetener

Directions:

1. Line a small baking sheet with parchment paper.

2. In an even, single layer arrange the chopped cherries on the baking sheet.

3. Melt the coconut oil using a microwave. Stir in the cocoa powder and cola-flavored sweetener drops and entirely combine.

4. Pour the mixture evenly over the chopped cherries. Freeze until set.

5. Break into shards before enjoying.

Caramel-Cola Popcorn

On your next movie night, take your popcorn to the next level with the irresistible flavors of sweet caramel and cola. Be warned though, you may want to make two batches, this snack goes quick!

Servings: 4

Total Time: 45min

Ingredients:

- 2 bags plain microwaveable popcorn (popped)
- ¾ cup salted butter
- ⅓ cup cola (room temperature)
- 1 cup brown sugar
- ¼ cup light corn syrup

Directions:

1. Preheat the main oven to 300 degrees F. Cover a baking sheet with parchment paper.

2. Add the popped popcorn to a large bowl.

3. Melt together the butter, cola, sugar, and corn syrup in a saucepan over moderate heat. Bring the mixture to a boil and cook for 4 minutes without stirring.

4. Pour the caramel over the popcorn. Toss until the popcorn is coated evenly in the caramel.

5. Transfer the popcorn to the baking sheet and bake in the oven for just over 20 minutes.

6. Allow to cool before serving.

Cherry Cola Jellies

Chewy little jelly candies with the yummy flavor of cherry cola will be loved by kids and grownups alike!

Servings: 24

Total Time: 4hours 15min

Ingredients:

- 1¼ cups cola (room temperature)
- 1 (3.4 ounce) box cherry-flavored jello mix

Directions:

1. Line an 8 inch square baking tin with a double layer of aluminum foil.

2. Add the cola to a bowl and warm in the microwave for 2 minutes until boiling.

3. Whisk the jello powder into the cola until it dissolves. Pour the mixture into the prepared baking tin.

4. Chill the mixture for 3-4 hours.

5. Using the foil, lift the jello out of the tin. Peel away the foil. Slice the slab into cubes and enjoy!

Chocolate Cola Mousse Pots

Cloud-light mousse with its fluffy texture and the sweet chocolatey flavor is the perfect dessert for all the family. What's more, served in individual cups, it's the perfect choice for parties and informal get-togethers.

Servings: 6

Total Time: 50min

Ingredients:

- 5 tbsp cold water
- 2 (¼ ounce) sachets unflavored gelatin powder
- 1 large whole egg
- 1 large egg yolk
- ¼ cup granulated sugar
- ½ cup semi-sweet choc chips
- 1 cup diet cola (room temperature)
- ¾ cup heavy cream
- Whipped cream (for serving)

Directions:

1. Add the water to a small bowl and sprinkle over the gelatin. Set aside for a few minutes to dissolve.

2. Using a double boiler, heat together the egg, yolk, and granulated sugar. Whisk to combine and gently cook for several minutes until creamy and thick.

3. Using a double boiler set up, warm the gelatin mixture until liquid and add to the egg mixture. Stir gently to combine.

4. Melt the choc chips using a microwave. Fold the melted chocolate into the egg/gelatine mixture and whisk in the cola. Chill the mixture for 10-15 minutes, removing 2-3 times to stir.

5. In the meantime, whisk the heavy cream until it can hold stiff peaks.

6. Fold the cream into the chilled chocolate mixture. Divide the mousse between 6 individual cups. Cover and chill for half an hour.

7. Lastly, top each portion with a dollop of whipped cream before serving.

Cola Cupcakes with Vanilla Frosting

Who doesn't love a classic cupcake? Especially when it consists of airy cocoa and cola sponge and topped with a swirl of sweet vanilla frosting. Decorate with maraschino cherries for a pretty finishing touch.

Servings: 15

Total Time: 1hour

Ingredients:

- Nonstick cooking spray

Cupcakes:

- 2 cups cola (room temperature)
- ½ cup unsalted butter (chipped)
- 1 cup dark, unsweetened cocoa powder
- 1¼ cups granulated sugar
- ½ cup brown sugar
- 2 cups all-purpose flour
- 1 tsp salt
- 1¼ tsp baking soda
- 2 eggs

Frosting:

- 1½ cups heavy cream
- ½ tsp vanilla essence
- 2 tbsp sugar powder
- 15 maraschino cherries (to decorate)

Directions:

1. Preheat your main oven to 325 degrees F. Spritz the wells of 2 cupcakes tin with nonstick cooking spray.

2. In a saucepan over moderate heat, melt together the cola, butter, and cocoa powder. Add the granulated and brown sugar to the pan and whisk until it has dissolved. Take the pan off the heat. Allow to cool.

3. In a bowl, combine the baking soda, flour, and salt.

4. In a second small bowl, beat the eggs, then add them to the flour mixture. Next, fold the cola mixture into the flour until incorporated. Do not worry if the batter is a little lumpy.

5. Pour the batter equally into the cupcake tins and bake in the oven for 20 minutes. Rotate the cupcake tins halfway through baking. Allow the cupcakes cooling completely before frosting.

6. In the meantime, prepare the frosting. Add the heavy cream, vanilla essence, and powdered sugar to an electric mixer. Beat until the mixture can hold medium peaks. Transfer the frosting to a piping bag and frost the cooled cupcakes.

7. Top each cupcake with a maraschino cherry before serving.

Diet Cola Trifle

For those that haven't encountered this British classic before, trifle is a pudding-like dessert that brings together layers of sweet ingredients with varying flavors and textures. This particular trifle features cola-flavored sponge, milky vanilla pudding, and air-light whipped cream.

Servings: 6-8

Total Time: 2hours 30min

Ingredients:

- Nonstick cooking spray
- 1 (15¼ ounces) box yellow cake mix
- 12 ounces diet cola (room temperature)
- 1 (1 ounce) sachet sugar-free instant vanilla pudding mix
- 2 cups skimmed milk
- 8 ounces whipped topping

Directions:

1. Preheat the main oven to the temperature indicated on the cake mix box.

2. Spritz a 13x9 inch baking tin with nonstick cooking spray.

3. Beat together the cake mix and diet cola until smooth. Pour the batter into the baking tin and bake in the oven according to the manufacturer's instructions.

4. Allow the cake to cool before cutting into 1 inch cubes.

5. Whisk together the pudding mix and milk until combined. Keep chilled until ready to assemble.

6. Arrange one-third of cooled cake cubes in the base of a trifle dish in an even layer, followed by a third of the pudding and a third of whipped topping. Repeat the layers two more times until the ingredients are used up.

7. Chill for 1-2 hours before serving.

Frosted Cola Cookies

Soft, chewy cookies with a fluffy and butter cola-flavored frosting are an irresistible treat for all the family; big and small!

Servings: 30

Total Time: 1hour

Ingredients:

Cookies:

- 2½ cups all-purpose flour
- ½ tsp bicarb of soda
- ½ tsp salt
- ½ cup butter (softened)
- ¾ cup granulated sugar
- ½ cup brown sugar
- 1 medium egg (at room temperature)
- ½ tsp of baking powder
- 2 tbsp vanilla essence
- ½ cup cola (at room temperature)

Frosting:

- 8 tbsp butter (at room temperature)
- 4 cups confectioner's sugar
- ¼ cup cola (at room temperature)

Directions:

1. Preheat a main oven to 350 degrees F. Cover a cookie sheet with parchment paper.

2. In a bowl, combine the flour, bicarb of soda, salt, and baking powder.

3. In a second bowl, beat together the butter, granulated sugar, and brown sugar until fluffy; this should take approximately 2 minutes.

4. Beat the egg, vanilla essence, and coca cola into the butter until just incorporated.

5. Beat the flour into the butter mixture a half cup at a time until the dough is just combined.

6. Using a 1½ tablespoon scoop, spoon the dough onto the cookie sheets, around 2 inches apart.

7. Place in the oven and bake for approximately 12 minutes, rotate the cookie sheet halfway through baking.

8. Take the cookies out of the oven. Allow sitting for a couple of minutes before transferring them to a metal baking rack to cool.

9. In the meantime, prepare the frosting. Beat together the butter and 1 cup powdered sugar until fluffy.

10. Beat the cola into the frosting before mixing in the remaining confectioner's sugar, 1 cup at a time. Spread the frosting over the cooled cookies.

11. Enjoy.

Glazed Cocoa Cola Cake

Using buttermilk in cake batter creates a super soft and moist sponge, which makes this cake the perfect treat to serve alongside afternoon tea or morning coffee.

Servings: 14

Total Time: 50min

Ingredients:

- Butter (to grease)

Cake:

- 2 cups all-purpose flour
- 1 tsp bicarb of soda
- ½ tsp ground cinnamon
- 2 cups sugar
- ½ tsp salt
- 12 ounces cola
- ¼ cup baking cocoa powder
- 1 cup salted butter (cubed)
- ½ cup buttermilk
- 2 eggs (at room temperature)
- 1 tsp vanilla essence

Glaze:

- 12 ounces cola (room temperature)
- ¼ cup baking cocoa powder
- ½ cup butter (cubed)
- 4 cups powdered sugar

Directions:

1. Preheat a main oven to 350 degrees F. Grease a 9x13 inch baking tin.

2. Combine the flour, bicarb of soda, cinnamon, sugar, and salt in a bowl.

3. Add the cola, cocoa powder, and butter to a saucepan over moderately high heat and bring to a boil while stirring occasionally.

4. Pour the cola mixture into the bowl with the dry ingredients and stir to combine.

5. In a small bowl, beat together the buttermilk, eggs, and vanilla essence. Fold into the cola/flour until incorporated.

6. Pour the batter into the baking tin and bake for just under half an hour until the center is entirely set.

7. When the cake has only 15 minutes of baking time remaining, prepare the glaze. Bring the cola to a boil in a small saucepan, heat for 12-15 minutes until you have around a ½ cup of syrup.

8. Stir the cocoa powder and butter into the syrup until the butter has melted, and whisk in the powdered sugar until smooth and lump-free.

9. Drizzle the glaze over the cake while warm. Allow the glaze to cool and set before slicing and serving.

Gourmet Citrus Homemade Cola Snow Cones

Make your own cola! These snow cones are a fun, frozen treat with natural, homemade citrus-cola flavoring to help you cool off on those hotter days.

Servings: 8-10

Total Time: 1hour

Ingredients:

- 1¼ cups water
- ½ cup brown sugar
- 13½ ounces superfine sugar
- 1 tsp fresh ginger (grated)
- 1 cinnamon stick
- ½ tsp coriander seeds
- ½ star anise
- ¼ tsp dried lavender
- ⅛ tsp fresh nutmeg (grated)
- Zest and juice of 1 lime, 1 lemon, and 1 orange
- ½ tsp citric acid
- Scrapings of ½ a vanilla bean
- 21 ounces crushed ice

Directions:

1. To a saucepan over moderate heat, add the water, brown sugar, superfine sugar, ginger, cinnamon stick, coriander seeds, star anise, lavender, and nutmeg. Stir and heat until the sugars dissolve and the mixture is simmering. Turn the heat down to low. Simmer for 5 minutes.

2. Take the syrup off the heat, then allow it to cool for an hour before stirring in the citrus juices, zest, citric acid, and vanilla.

3. Strain the syrup, discard solids, and chill the syrup until cool*.

4. To serve, divide the crushed ice between serving cups and drizzle with an equal amount of prepared syrup.

*Prepared syrup can keep in the refrigerator for up to 28 days

Handmade Cherry Cola Sorbet

Great news! You don’t need a high-priced ice cream machine to make this fruity and refreshing cherry cola sorbet.

Servings: 6

Total Time: 6hours 20min

Ingredients:

- 24 ounces pitted, frozen dark cherries (thawed)
- ½ cup fresh dark cherry juice
- 1 cup cola (room temperature)
- Juice of 1 medium lemon
- ½ cup simple sugar syrup

Directions:

1. Add cherries to a food processor and blitz until smooth. Transfer to a bowl along with the dark cherry juice, cola, lemon juice, and sugar syrup. Stir until combined.

2. Pour the mixture into ice cube trays. Freeze until solid.

3. Add the frozen sorbet cubes to a food processor and blitz until slushy. Pour the mixture into a freezer-safe container, then freeze until more firm before serving.

Maple Cola Pancake Stack

Golden pancakes flavored with sweet cola are stacked and drizzled with maple syrup for a yummy brunch-time treat or dessert.

Servings: 6-8

Total Time: 20min

Ingredients:

- 1 medium egg
- 1 cup whole milk
- ¼ cup cola (room temperature)
- 1 cup self-raising flour
- Nonstick cooking spray
- Maple syrup (for serving)

Directions:

1. Place a skillet over moderate heat to warm.

2. In a bowl, beat together the egg, milk, cola, and flour.

3. Spritz the skillet with nonstick cooking spray.

4. Pour ladleful of the batter into the skillet. Cook until the surface begins to bubble, flip, and cook until the second side is golden, and repeat until all of the batter is cooked.

5. Stack the cooked pancakes, drizzle with plenty of maple syrup and serve straight away!

Nutty Walnut and Cola Fudge

Smooth and creamy fudge with crunchy walnut pieces is a flavor and texture sensation.

Servings: 54

Total Time: 3hours 30min

Ingredients:

- Nonstick cooking spray
- ¾ cup butter
- ⅔ cup evaporated milk
- 3 cups granulated sugar
- 7½ ounces cola (room temperature)
- 12 ounces semi-sweet choc chips
- 7 ounces marshmallow crème
- 1¼ cups chopped walnuts

Directions:

1. Line a 9x13 inch baking tin with parchment and spritz with nonstick cooking spray.

2. In a saucepan over moderate heat, melt the butter. Stir in the evaporated milk, sugar, and cola. Heat to a boil, stirring continually for 5 minutes.

3. Take the pan off the heat and stir in the choc chips and marshmallow crème until smooth and incorporated.

4. Fold in 1 cup of the chopped walnuts.

5. Pour the mixture into the baking tin and sprinkle over the remaining walnuts.

6. Chill for 2-3 hours until set.

7. Slice into squares and serve.

Rich Cola Brownies

Moist, fudgy, and rich in intense chocolate flavor - just how a good brownie should be! Serve with a glass of milk while still warm for the ultimate and indulgent treat.

Servings: 12

Total Time: 45min

Ingredients:

- 1¼ cups all-purpose flour
- ⅔ cup cocoa powder
- 1⅔ cup granulated sugar
- ½ tsp salt
- ½ tsp baking powder
- 12 ounces cola (room temperature)

Directions:

1. Preheat a main oven to 350 degrees F. Line a baking tin with aluminum foil and place the oven rack in the center of the oven.

2. Combine the flour, cocoa powder, sugar, and salt in a bowl. A little at a time, whisk in the cola until the mixture comes together as a smooth batter.

3. Pour the batter into the baking tin. Bake in the oven for half an hour. Allow to cool before slicing into squares and serving.

4. Enjoy.

Sticky Date and Cola Pudding with Bourbon-Caramel Sauce

Sticky date pudding is a much-loved classic in the UK and is one of Gordon Ramsay's signature dishes. Give this British dessert an American update with smoky bourbon and sweet cola.

Servings: 8-10

Total Time: 2hours 10min

Ingredients:

Caramel Sauce:

- 3½ ounces milk chocolate
- 8¾ ounces brown sugar
- 8¾ ounces salted butter
- 1 cup heavy cream
- ⅓ cup bourbon
- 1½ tsp sea salt

Pudding:

- 4⅓ ounces pitted prunes (chopped)
- 4⅓ ounces pitted dates (chopped)
- 1½ cups cola (room temperature)
- 4⅓ ounces brown sugar
- 3 ounces butter
- 2 large eggs
- ⅓ cup bourbon
- 1 tsp vanilla essence
- 1 tsp baking powder
- 11⅓ ounces self-raising flour
- 1 tsp bicarbonate of soda
- 1 tsp sea salt

Directions:

1. First, prepare the caramel sauce: Add the milk chocolate, brown sugar, salted butter, and heavy cream to a saucepan over moderate heat and while stirring warm gently until melted.

2. Take the pan off the heat. Whisk in the bourbon and salt and pour a little of the sauce into the bottom of a baking dish and chill for 20 minutes. Set the remaining caramel sauce to one side.

3. To make the pudding, preheat the main oven to 325 degrees F. Add the prunes and dates to a saucepan along with the cola and place over low heat for 5 minutes.

4. In the meantime, beat together the brown sugar and butter using an electric mixer until fluffy.

5. Beat in eggs one at a time followed by the bourbon, vanilla essence, baking powder, and self-raising flour until combined.

6. Stir the bicarbonate of soda and salt into the hot dates and prunes. Fold the fruit into the butter/flour mixture until incorporated.

7. Pour the pudding mix into the prepared baking tin and bake for 40 minutes until cooked through.

8. Heat the set-aside caramel sauce from Step 2 and pour over the pudding while it is still warm.

9. Slice and enjoy.

Whiskey 'n Cola Truffles

With a generous glug of whiskey, these boozy, rich truffles pack a punch! They would make a thoughtful food gift for your whiskey 'n cola loving friends.

Servings: 24

Total Time: 14hour 30min

Ingredients:

Truffles:

- 15 ounces cola (room temperature)
- ¼ cup butter
- ½ cup heavy cream
- 1 tsp vanilla essence
- ¼ cup brown sugar
- Pinch salt
- 12 ounces semi-sweet choc chips
- ½ cup dark choc chips
- ¼ cup whiskey of choice

Coating:

- ½ cup semi-sweet choc chips
- 2 tbsp coconut oil

Directions:

1. Pour the cola into a saucepan and place over moderately high heat, bring to a boil. Boil until the liquid reduces to a ¼ cup.

2. Add the butter to the reduced cola and stir until the butter melts. Next, stir in the heavy cream, vanilla essence, brown sugar, and salt. Return the mixture to a boil and take off the heat.

3. Add the choc chips to a bowl. Pour the cola mixture over the choc chips and stir until the mixture is melted and silky. Allow to cool before stirring in the whiskey. Cover the bowl with plastic wrap and freeze for half an hour.

4. Cover a cookie sheet with wax paper. Grease the paper.

5. Take the bowl out of the freezer. Stir the mixture well.

6. A tablespoon at a time, drop the mixture onto the cookie sheet. Return to the freezer for 15-20 minutes until firm.

7. Prepare the coating: Melt the semi-sweet choc chips together with the coconut oil in a microwave and stir until silky. Make sure the mixture is not too hot before dipping each truffle in the melted chocolate to coat. Return the truffles to the cookie sheet.

8. Transfer the truffles to the fridge to chill until set before serving.

Author's Afterthoughts

I would like to express my deepest thanks to you, the reader, for making this investment in one my books. I cherish the thought of bringing the love of cooking into your home.

With so much choice out there, I am grateful you decided to Purch this book and read it from beginning to end.

Please let me know by submitting an Amazon review if you enjoyed this book and found it contained valuable information to help you in your culinary endeavors. Please take a few minutes to express your opinion freely and honestly. This will help others make an informed decision on purchasing and provide me with valuable feedback.

Thank you for taking the time to review!

Christina Tosch

About the Author

Christina Tosch is a successful chef and renowned cookbook author from Long Grove, Illinois. She majored in Liberal Arts at Trinity International University and decided to pursue her passion of cooking when she applied to the world renowned Le Cordon Bleu culinary school in Paris, France. The school was lucky to recognize the immense talent of this chef and she excelled in her courses, particularly Haute Cuisine. This skill was recognized and rewarded by several highly regarded Chicago restaurants, where she was offered the prestigious position of head chef.

Christina and her family live in a spacious home in the Chicago area and she loves to grow her own vegetables and herbs in the garden she lovingly cultivates on her sprawling estate. Her and her husband have two beautiful children, 3 cats, 2 dogs and a parakeet they call Jasper. When Christina is not hard at work creating beautiful meals for Chicago's elite, she is hard at work writing engaging e-books of which she has sold over 1500.

Make sure to keep an eye out for her latest books that offer helpful tips, clear instructions and witty anecdotes that will bring a smile to your face as you read!

Made in the USA
Las Vegas, NV
03 December 2022